Original title:
The Juicy Kiss

Copyright © 2025 Creative Arts Management OÜ
All rights reserved.

Author: Rafael Sterling
ISBN HARDBACK: 978-1-80586-453-0
ISBN PAPERBACK: 978-1-80586-925-2

Lips Like Ripe Fruit

Your lips are cherries, oh so sweet,
A playful bite is quite the treat.
I lean in close, prepared to munch,
On juicy moments, it's quite the crunch.

Sticky giggles fill the air,
A fruit salad's just too rare.
With each caress, a splashy sound,
In this orchard, love's profound.

Nectar on My Tongue

A sip of sweetness, I can taste,
Your laughter, never goes to waste.
Like honey drips on sunny days,
In silly games, we always play.

With playful jabs and smiles so wide,
In this flavor fest, we glide.
Your juice is bliss I can't ignore,
Let's savor more, oh please, encore!

Sweet Surrender in Twilight

As stars twinkle, we dive in deep,
Your lips, a promise – oh, so sweet.
Under the moon, let's make a scene,
A sugary dance, oh so serene.

With whispered jokes and silly sighs,
Each moment bursts like fireflies.
In twilight's glow, we chuckle and sway,
Surrendering to laughter's play.

Tangy Whispers of Passion

With every nibble, flavors meld,
In tangy whispers, stories held.
Your smile is citrus, bright and bold,
In our comedy, love unfolds.

We tango under a slicing lime,
Life's a fruit bowl, oh so prime.
With playful pecks and citrus zest,
In silly moments, we're truly blessed.

Blooming Whispers

In the garden where laughter grows,
Petals flutter with silly prose,
Bees buzz around, a comedy show,
Nectar's sweet, as everyone knows.

A bumblebee winks, what a sight!
Dancing away through the golden light.
Flowers blush, feeling quite bold,
Tickles of sunshine, a joy to behold.

With every sip of that sugary dew,
Giggles erupt when the daisies pursue.
A moth and a ladybug start a chase,
Spinning in circles, oh what a race!

In this whimsical world, let's be a fool,
Where nature's secret becomes a cool tool.
So slip on your shoes, take a gleeful leap,
And taste the delight, but don't take a peep!

Surprising Sparks

On a picnic, packed full of snacks,
We found a treasure, oh what a max!
A jar of pickles, those crunchy delights,
Brought out some giggles and dizzying heights.

In the corner, ants threw a ballet,
While squirrels dressed up in a grand display.
Each silly dance, a spark of pure cheer,
Even the sun grinned, bringing us near.

A mouthful of mustard went straight to my nose,
Made everyone laugh, as the condiment goes.
Chasing my sandwich, the dog took a dive,
Rolling in laughter, oh how we thrive!

So here's to the fun, so vibrant and bright,
Moments of joy, like stars in the night.
Let's embrace surprise, with each little quirk,
And dance with the sparks, for life's a great work!

Citrus Whispers

A wedge of lemon on my day,
Teasing soft in a zesty way.
With every twist a giggle grows,
Sour secrets nobody knows.

A tango danced with orange peels,
Each little bite a burst of feels.
Lime laughs linger in the air,
Pulls us close without a care.

Forbidden Fruit

An apple gleams with mischief bright,
Tempting tongues in the moonlight.
Biting into scandal's core,
Sips of sweetness leave us wanting more.

Banana slips on laughter's lane,
Chasing joy in playful gain.
Pineapple dreams and cherry pies,
Giggles crisp as the sunlit skies.

Sweet Surrender

Grapes of joy cascade like rain,
Rolling laughter, fun unchained.
Juicy joys drip down our chins,
As sticky sweetness always wins.

Peachy winks and taffy twists,
In this game, no one resists.
With every taste, a silly grin,
In fruit-filled games, we all dive in.

Juices of Autumn

Pumpkin spice and silly cheer,
Squashes giggle, loud and clear.
Each sip a dance of fleeting fun,
In harvest moons we all have won.

Cranberries tease with tart delight,
While cider swirls in the chilly night.
Sipping bold with friends, we boast,
In fruity antics, we all toast!

Tangled in Tastes

A berry burst upon her lips,
With cherry twirls in quickened sips.
To nibble near, the flavors mix,
A chorus of sweet, sticky tricks.

Banana peels and grape confetti,
A fruity dance, oh so petty.
With laughter bubbling, taste buds sing,
We're tangled up in this wild fling.

Abundant Affection

With each bite, a giggle flies,
Melons wink with sunny skies.
A splash of juice, a playful mess,
Her smile gleamed, sheer happiness.

The mango swirls, a vibrant tease,
An amorous taste that aims to please.
With every nibble, joy expands,
Embracing sweetness with eager hands.

Ecstatic Elixirs

A potion brewed in laughter's light,
With zestful sips from day to night.
Kiwi dreams in every pour,
We guzzle fun, then ask for more.

She grins as passion bubbles high,
A splash of lime in a twinkling eye.
We stumble, fumble, drip and shout,
These elixirs fuel our playful bout.

Ephemeral Delights

Each fleeting taste, a fleeting cheer,
With kisses quick, the end is near.
A swirl of flavors meets the tongue,
This dance of joy, forever young.

In sprightly jests, we trade a bite,
With candy hopes, our hearts take flight.
So let's embrace this tasty spree,
For fleeting joys keep us carefree.

Sweet Serenades

In the garden of laughter, we meet,
With a fruit that's ripe, oh so sweet.
We giggle and squirm, a playful tease,
Another bite in the summer breeze.

With a splash of cream and a wink,
I raise my glass, you give a blink.
Silly faces, sticky hands galore,
What a fun mess on the kitchen floor!

Moments of Extravagance

In a world of flavors, we dive right in,
Chocolate sauce drips, oh what a sin!
With giggles and squawks, our tongues all dance,
Daring bites to give love a chance.

A dribble here, a splash right there,
Laughter erupts, taking all care.
Mustache of syrup, so grand and bold,
Sweet mischief shared, treasures untold.

Bliss in Every Drop

A sip of joy as we clink our cups,
In this sweet moment, everyone's up.
Our cheeks are flushed, like cherries in bloom,
The flavor's a party, it lights up the room.

With each little drip, we can't help but giggle,
Sticky and funny, it makes our hearts wiggle.
A splash on your nose makes us laugh till we cry,
In this juicy conquest, we're never too shy!

Wondrous Flavors

In a carnival of tastes, we jest and play,
Mixing flavors in a most absurd way.
Banana and pickle, oh what a sight,
Each bite is a chuckle, a sheer delight.

Spinning like tops, we join the parade,
With every odd combo, our worries fade.
This fruit-filled fiasco brings joy to our day,
In our flavorful chaos, let's laugh all the way!

Vivid Impressions

A smacker on the cheek, so bold,
Like raspberries swirled with honey, pure gold.
It leaves me grinning, no need to disguise,
A flavored surprise, oh what a prize!

With lips sticky like candy, what a treat,
Laughter bubbles up, oh, isn't that sweet?
Sipping soda while sharing giggles galore,
Hoping for more, and then some more!

A choco-mustache, what a sight it does make,
With each buttery bite, I start to quake.
Wondrous concoctions dance on my tongue,
In this zany moment, I feel so young!

So here's to the moments, both quirky and bright,
Under rainbow sprinkles, we revel in delight.
With each scrumptious cuddle, we just might miss,
This laughter, this joy, the taste of pure bliss!

Overflowing with Bliss

A splash of sweetness, oh what a sight,
Like whipped cream clouds on a starry night.
These playful encounters, a wink and a grin,
In this carnival of flavors, let the fun begin!

Banana peels slide, whoosh, here I go,
With my bouncing heart and a silly show.
Bubblegum laughter, it fills the air,
As we wobble and wobble, without a care!

Juicy dribbles down, oh what a mess!
Syrup-covered giggles, who could guess?
We stumble through puddles, oh, what a fuss,
In this field of cherries, why make a fuss?

With each sticky smooch, the zany vibe grows,
Kisses of jelly, like fireworks, it shows.
In this grand adventure, we cavalcade bliss,
Through flavors and laughter, oh, yes, oh yes!

Taste of the Unattainable

I reach for the pear, but it's just out of hand,
Like trying to catch bubbles that float on demand.
The fruit whispers secrets that dance in the air,
But I chase it in vain, it's never quite fair.

A slice of ambrosia on my hopeful plate,
With each little bite, I feel like it's fate.
Yet somehow, it slips just as soon as it's near,
This scrum-diddly-umptiousness, drawing me near!

Chocolate fountains flow like dreams wild and free,
But gravity plays tricks as I reach for thee.
Fruit loops and giggles all bounce from my hand,
While I daydream of flavors I can't understand.

Still, each bubbly thought sends me soaring high,
Chasing sweet memories, oh my, oh my!
In this circus of tastes, come take a ride,
For in every attempt, we find joy worldwide!

Liquid Comfort

A sip of the funkiest, fizziest brew,
Bubbles tickle my nose, oh, what a view!
With each quirky gulp, I'm thrown in a whirl,
Like a fizzy tornado sends my mind in a twirl!

Candy-flavored straws stretch higher than skies,
Swirling rainbows reflect in my eyes.
Each swallow a giggle, a bubbly delight,
I float on the sweetness, oh, what a flight!

A pool of froth, melt away my blues,
In this carnival cup, I can't quite lose.
Liquid happiness spills all around,
In this sippable treasure, pure joy I have found.

So raise up a toast to the flavors so bold,
With laughter and fun, there's magic to hold.
In every silly fizz, let our hearts soar,
For in this bright moment, who could want more?

Savoring Each Moment's Bite

In the garden of sweet delight,
I found a berry, oh so bright.
With laughter bubbling like champagne,
I tasted joy, oh what a gain!

The ants formed lines, in perfect rows,
They danced and twirled, in funny shows.
Each nibble brought a silly grin,
As juicy sweetness swept me in!

Refreshing Breeze of Connection

A breeze tickled my silly hair,
With fruit-filled dreams, I took to air.
The scent of oranges filled the sky,
I laughed so hard, I nearly cried.

The ripened fruits had quite the flair,
They whispered jokes, light as the air.
Each chuckle echoed in the space,
Connecting hearts in this fun race!

Tasting the Stars Above

In a night covered with whipped cream,
I reached for stars, what a wild dream!
Each twinkle burst like a citrus blast,
Laughter sparkled, a joyful contrast.

With cosmic treats from way up high,
A melon moon caught my eye.
I bit and giggled at the taste,
As stardust dripped and twirled with haste!

Luscious Secrets Beneath the Surface

Beneath the leaves, a treasure lies,
A hidden snack that catches eyes.
With playful hands, I dug around,
Unveiling giggles underground.

The roots they whispered, secrets sweet,
To dig them up was such a treat!
I chomped a bite, the laughter grew,
As flavors mingled, fresh and new!

Quenching Thirsts

A fruit fell down, quite out of place,
It splattered sweet juice, oh, what a face!
Everyone laughed, their giggles took flight,
As they wiped sticky hands, a sugary sight.

In the garden bright, we danced with glee,
Mangoes and melons, oh can't you see?
We raced for the fountain, a splashy delight,
Guzzling down bliss, from morning till night.

Serendipity in a Squeeze

Lemon zest lingers on the tip of my nose,
A citrusy prank as the laughter just flows.
With every squirt, a squeal fills the air,
We slip on the ground, but who really cares?

A grapefruit bounces, no slow motion here,
It lands on my pal, filled with fresh cheer.
All smiles and giggles, a salad of fun,
Squeezing joy out of life, we just can't be done!

Luscious Labyrinths

In a maze made of berries, we danced round and round,
Each bite a giggle, our laughter profound.
Cherries were chatter, raspberries rhyme,
Wandering fruit fields, losing all track of time.

With each juicy nibble, we found new delight,
A blueberry bush gave us quite a fright!
It moaned and it groaned, oh what a tease,
A fruit-filled adventure, we did just as we please!

Delicate Temptations

A peach on the desk, au naturel shine,
With every small nibble, so perfectly fine.
But the pit had a plan, it rolled off the edge,
We all burst out laughing, oh what a pledge!

With cupcakes and frosting, we hatched a great scheme,
An icing catapult; oh what a dream!
A dash of the sprinkles, the sugar cascade,
In this fruit-filled world, let's boldly parade!

Radiant Rapture

A burst of sweetness, oh what glee,
When lips collide, life's jubilee.
Like candy rain on a summer's day,
Each playful peck makes worries sway.

In the park, two pigeons collide,
With a peck that's full of wild pride.
Laughter trailing in the soft breeze,
Love's silly dance, sure to tease.

Sipping soda with a fizzy pop,
With cherry lips, we can't stop.
Giggles echo as we share our treat,
Messy faces, oh what a feat!

In a world where flavors mix,
We create our own little tricks.
With every smirk and every grin,
The joy of taste is where we begin.

Garden of Delights

In a garden where we bloom so bright,
Nectar drips in the warm sunlight.
Petals scatter with each playful place,
Sticky fingers and a sweet embrace.

Bumblebees buzz, oh such a hum,
As we search for the flavors, oh so fun.
With laughter ripe like fruit on the vine,
We bite and nibble, oh feeling fine!

Thorns may prick in our silly chase,
Yet we savor each delightful taste.
A pear, a peach, a funny face,
As juice runs down at a rapid pace.

With giggles shared under leafy green,
Every moment bursts like a scene.
In this garden, our laughter sings,
As love's absurdity takes to wings.

Embraced by Flavor

Two mimosas clink with a bubbly cheer,
As we toast to joy that's always near.
Sipping sunshine from glasses bright,
With playful banter, we take flight.

Chocolate drips, oh where to bite?
A silly mess, what pure delight!
With whipped cream smiles, we aim to please,
Dancing flavors that tease and squeeze.

Tasting cake like a sweet parade,
With laughter layered, never fades.
In every crumb, a giggle hides,
As flavor conquers and joy resides.

So come and munch on this mirthful spree,
Where we're embraced by taste, you see.
With each shared plate and silly jest,
The flavor of fun truly is the best.

Velvet on the Palette

Soft and rich, a velvet hue,
Licking flavors from me to you.
With every swirl, a kiss of cream,
Savoring life like a funky dream.

A sprinkle here, a dash of fun,
Chocolate laughs when the tasting's done.
Bright fruit dips in a silly dance,
Each bite invites a goofy prance.

Minty whispers that tickle the tongue,
Songs of sweetness that we have sung.
Dripping laughter like melting cones,
Sharing sillies, our happy tones.

Painted taste in colors so bright,
Every morsel feels just right.
With giggles laced like frosted bliss,
Oh! These moments, we dare not miss!

Irresistible Flavor of You

A splash of peach, a hint of zest,
Your grin is candy, I must confess.
With every chuckle, sweetness blooms,
Like chocolate secrets in cozy rooms.

Your laughter's syrup, sticky and bright,
Makes mundane moments feel just right.
Like lemonade served on a sunny day,
You squeeze my heart in the funniest way.

The Art of Flavorful Encounters

We met in the kitchen, pots were ablaze,
Our playful banter ignited the craze.
You tossed in some humor, a dash of fun,
Cooking up joys until we were done.

Your words, like spices, twinkle and twirl,
I savor each moment, let my heart whirl.
We blend and mix, a recipe rare,
Together in laughter, we float on the air.

Serenade of Sweet Temptation

Under the moon, we had our fun,
With jellybeans dancing, we spun and spun.
Your jokes are toppings, so silly and grand,
Sprinkling magic like fine fairy sand.

With whispers like licorice, sweet and so sly,
You lure me in with every sly eye.
Each playful poke, a flavor unique,
In this sugary bond, we both feel the peak.

Luscious Echoes of our Dance

We twirled together, feet took flight,
Like a candy store bursting with light.
Your steps are jelly, wobbly and fun,
As we laugh and giggle, our race has begun.

We pirouette through flavors, sweet and surreal,
With every spin, you're the best meal.
In a world of sprinkles, I crave your kiss,
Your playful whispers, I can't resist.

Luscious Encounters

In the garden, I did sneak,
A fruit so plump, a kiss I seek.
With juice that drips, oh what a sight,
I laughed so hard, it felt just right.

I went for bites, with cheeks so full,
The flavor burst, it was quite the pull.
I rolled and tumbled, what a spree,
This fruity dance, just you and me.

I smushed a peach, it splashed so bold,
My shirt now stained, a tale retold.
Yet giggles echoed, in sunlit park,
These luscious laughs, igniting spark.

Nature's jest, so sweet and light,
In each bright bite, pure delight.
It's not just fruit, but joy we find,
A silly kiss, so unconfined.

Essence of Euphoria

In a world of ripe delight,
A splash of laughter took to flight.
With zest so bright, it tickled me,
A citrus kiss, oh can you see?

I squeezed a lemon, oh what a show,
A pucker dance, I didn't know!
With giggles shared in sunlit gleam,
These funny moments, like a dream.

A berry burst, a juicy tease,
I slipped and fell, oh gracious ease!
Raspberries stuck, like love's embrace,
These playful kisses, my laughing grace.

In the fruit bowl, chaos reigns,
With each wild bite, joy entertains.
A splash of giggles, sweet delight,
These moments gleam, our hearts in flight.

Fruitful Embrace

Beneath the tree, a wild affair,
With juicy fruits, a kiss to share.
I chased a mango, golden round,
My silly jumps, a laughter sound.

A watermelon slice, such juicy fun,
We swiped and laughed, oh what a run!
With every bite, the juice would fly,
A sticky hug, beneath the sky.

In the orchard's midst, we'd spin and twirl,
Our fruity madness, a whirl and swirl.
A cherry fling, right in your face,
Splat! What a splash, a juicy grace!

With every noble fruit embraced,
These moments blessed, we've joy to taste.
With cheeky grins, our hearts collide,
In this embrace, where laughter glides.

Melting Moments

Ice cream scoops and fruit galore,
The sweet delight, who could ignore?
With sticky hands and laughter loud,
We dove right in, so joyous, proud.

A chocolate drizzle, oh what fun,
Melting kisses, two hearts spun.
Sprinkles flying, chaos reigns,
In each rich taste, our laughter gains.

Fruits all mixed in a colorful bowl,
With each new flavor, we felt it roll.
A slippery scoop, a giggly chase,
Our sweetened joy, a warm embrace.

As melting moments dance and play,
With fruity laughter, bright as day.
These silly bites, an open door,
To joyful hearts, forevermore.

Exquisite Juxtapositions

When blueberries meet with a pickle grin,
A taste explosion, where do I begin?
Sliced strawberries whisper secrets so sweet,
While onions skitter, dodging their feet.

Carrots dance with clementine flair,
Caught in a battle—a fruit and veggie affair.
A marshmallow floats in a puddle of jam,
While pickles tap dance, saying, "Oh, ma'am!"

Milkshakes jive with a splash of hot sauce,
In a blender twirl, with no sense of loss.
Gummy bears glide on a licorice night,
What a spectacle, oh what a sight!

In this bizarre feast, laughter's the rule,
A wacky buffet, oh how cool!
With each bite taken, my taste buds delight,
In a carnival of flavors, pure and bright.

Tango of Tantalizing Touches

A potato in heels does a shimmy and shake,
While salsa dips in—oh, what a mistake!
Tortillas twist like they're on a fun ride,
In this dance of flavors, where taste buds collide.

Cherries wear hats, all dressed up to sway,
As avocados watch—wrapped up in ballet.
Marshmallows prance, fluffy and proud,
While nuts form a chorus, singing out loud.

With each crunchy crunch and juicy delight,
The dessert waltzes under the moonlight.
A piñata bursts with laughter and cheer,
Tango of tastes, so fun to be here!

As we dip and we twirl in this culinary show,
Who knew a salad could put on such a glow?
In every bite, flavors narrated,
The dance of delight—so much celebrated!

Midnight Utopia

Under the stars, the snacks take a leap,
Popcorn pirouettes, while my chips make a sweep.
A fountain of chocolate bubbles up high,
As gummy worms wiggle and take to the sky.

Donuts are flipping like acrobatic pros,
As ice cream cones sing in sweet, creamy prose.
The marshmallow moon beams over the scene,
While burgers waltz, so grand and serene.

In this nighttime gala of flavors galore,
The laughter erupts; it's never a bore.
With chocolate sprinkles falling like stars,
We salute milkshakes from bright candy cars.

In midnight's embrace, we munch with delight,
A utopia crafted from flavors so bright.
As the clock ticks on, we savor the fun,
In this feast of laughter, we're never quite done!

The Dance of Sweetness

Candy canes twist in a comical dance,
While gelato giggles, giving life a chance.
Cookies do the cha-cha, all crispy and round,
In this merry fiesta, joy knows no bounds.

Chocolate chips wink from their cookie abode,
While lacey cupcakes take the party mode.
Whipped cream twirls on a slice of pie,
As tarts flicker flames in the dessert sky.

Fruit loops leap in a grand parade,
Dancing with joy, they're never afraid.
The sweetness of giggles fills up the air,
In a dance of deliciousness, nothing can compare.

So grab your fork and join in the fun,
In this sugary dance, we've only begun.
To taste is to laugh; to savor is bliss,
In this whimsical world, don't you dare miss!

Nectar on Tongues

In a garden full of cheer,
Flowers blush without a fear.
Bees are buzzing, oh so sly,
Hiding sweets, oh my, oh my!

Lips collide like fruit on trees,
Juices dripping in the breeze.
Sticky fingers and wild grins,
Where the laughter always begins.

Mango dances in the sun,
Two right steps, it's just pure fun.
Sticky situations, oh so grand,
Got fruit punch running through my hand!

Every smooch a daring quest,
Sour faces hidden jest.
Fruity flavors, wild delight,
Kissing like it's Friday night!

A Taste of Summer

Sun-kissed cheeks and playful minds,
Chasing after what one finds.
Lemonade and cheeky grins,
Summer heat, let chaos spin!

Scoops of laughter, ice cream fights,
Each cone drips on sunny heights.
With every scoop, we're tongue-tied,
Melted joy just cannot hide!

Candy colors, wild and bright,
Giggles echo through the night.
Sharing secrets, sticky hands,
Kisses sweeter than any plans.

In the midst of all the fun,
Dare to sneak a cheeky pun.
Every kiss a little bite,
Savored well until the night!

Pomegranate Secrets

Fruits that burst with every tease,
Whispers sweet like summer breeze.
Kisses with a tart surprise,
Giggling under watchful skies.

Seeds of joy, they spill about,
A playful query, what's that about?
Red and juicy, naughty flair,
Lips so close, we breathe the air.

Stains of laughter on our clothes,
Each conversation overflows.
Pomegranate's sweet escape,
Fruity kisses, endless shape!

With every bite, a daring shout,
Spilling secrets, laughter's route.
In this game of taste and fun,
We'll keep munching, never done!

Fleeting Flavors of Desire

Whisk me away on candy dreams,
Where sweetness flows in juicy streams.
A pop of flavor, a wink, a grin,
In this dance, we all shall spin!

Chocolate rivers, oh so fine,
Melting hearts with every line.
Whipped cream clouds that float and tease,
Where kisses melt with swooning ease.

Berry fumbles in the dusk,
Sipping softly, thrilling husk.
Strawberry shenanigans unfold,
Every moment, daring and bold.

Time slips by like melting ice,
Fleeting moments, perfect spice.
We'll chase these flavors more and more,
Till laughter echoes through the core!

Tango of Tasting

Two lips clash in a fruity dance,
Where flavors swirl and people prance.
A sip of sweet, a splash of zest,
In this taste tango, we are blessed.

With every nibble, giggles rise,
A swirl of cherries, oh what a surprise!
Each bite's a spin, a playful twirl,
Let's tango, darling, let's give it a whirl.

Fruits collide in a carnival of cheer,
The laughter bubbles with every smear.
Peaches and plums, such a silly plight,
They're bouncing off cheeks, oh what a sight!

So dip and dive in this flavor spree,
Let the party unfold, just you and me.
With every taste, we just can't resist,
Join the dance, in this fruit-filled mist!

Kissed by Sunshine

There's a glow that makes you grin,
A zesty spark on your chin.
Citrus joy, oh-so-bright,
A radiant flirt in the daylight.

Lemons giggle, oranges wink,
With every sip we start to think.
Sunshine beams in every drop,
Making this moment skip and hop.

A fruity embrace, sweet and bold,
Adventure wrapped in juicy gold.
Catch the rays with every taste,
A sunny kiss, never a waste.

So let's celebrate this vibrant scene,
With sunshine hugs, let's keep it keen.
In every splash, a burst of fun,
Together we laugh, united as one!

Sugary Echoes

Whispers of sweetness on the breeze,
Lively chuckles with playful ease.
Caramel drizzles, chocolate dips,
Echoes of laughter in fruity sips.

Marshmallow clouds float in the air,
Tickling noses, pure delight to share.
Sugar highs and candy smiles,
We savor the moment and walk for miles.

Every crunch brings a playful squeal,
Sharing giggles in a tasty reel.
Each bite a story, a laugh so bright,
In this sugary world, everything feels right.

So gather around for a sugary treat,
Let's celebrate life, oh-so-sweet.
With echoes of joy in every taste,
Let's sprinkle laughter, and never waste!

Tart Temptations

Tart little bites with a cheeky flair,
A puckered smile, with jokes to share.
Sour surprises in every crunch,
Each nibble brings a giggle and munch.

With zingy fruit, we dance and sway,
Like jesters playing in a fruity ballet.
Mouths twist and turn, oh what a thrill,
As we savor that tangy chill.

Raspberries tease with a tickle and laugh,
Each tart moment, a playful craft.
Laughter flows like a bubbling stream,
In this playful realm, we live the dream.

So join the fun, with a wink and a twist,
Tart temptations, you can't resist.
In every dodge, there's a smile to find,
Let's roll in the joy, leave worries behind!

Harvesting Electric Moments

In a garden of laughs where giggles grow,
We pluck zesty sparks, oh what a show!
Winking at bees buzzing on the vine,
Each tiny jolt feels oh-so divine.

Sunlight dances on cheeks like bright confetti,
With every tickle, we jump and get heady,
Catch me if you can, I'm a running fool,
Chasing the buzz like it's some kind of jewel.

Lemonade laughter flows from our lips,
As we dive into sweetness with fruity trips,
Electric vibes shock in a playful tease,
In this orchard of glee, we float like the breeze.

So let's harvest moments, sprinkle them fun,
With taste of wild joy, we're never outrun!
Our hearts in a splash, like fruits in a bowl,
This zany adventure is good for the soul.

Cherry Blossom Breath

A swirl of petals tickles my nose,
As I gaze at the blooms that sparkle and doze.
With every breath, I taste springtime delight,
In a giggling whirl, we dance in the light.

Two cherries chat, what a juicy affair,
They giggle and wink without a care,
In the breeze they flutter and hilariously shout,
"Taste me quick before summer's about!"

A picnic with pies that wiggle and plop,
Each bite a surprise, like bubbles that pop,
We're lost in the squabbles of sweet little dreams,
With laughter so bright, it bursts at the seams.

So let's twirl like petals, frolic and play,
In the orchard of whimsy, we'll frolic all day,
With fruity giggles and blossoms galore,
This cheeky romance leaves us wanting more!

Tangy Daydreams

In a meadow of zingers, where dreams dance and spin,
We sip on the sunshine and let the fun begin,
Lemon drops tumble from giggling clouds,
While we wade through laughter, swaying in crowds.

Our minds are a canvas, painted with flair,
Each zesty thought floats, great fluffy air,
So we skip through the tangy dew-kissed grass,
Collecting sweet smiles like moments that last.

Every twist and turn, we embrace the odd,
With a wink and a nudge, feeling quite prod,
The teasing of fruit flies gives us a tease,
As we break into hiccups, knees weak with glee.

So join this parade of flavor and cheer,
With a tingle of zest, let's make it all clear,
These daydreams we harvest, bold and bright,
In a whirlwind of fun, we laugh through the night.

Honeyed Words

Whispering secrets with a sticky sweet laugh,
Words drizzle down like syrupy math,
Each giggle we share turns the mundane sublime,
In this chatterbox world, we're dancing through rhyme.

Dialogues bubble like soda in flight,
Bubbling with fun, glowing oh-so bright,
With honeyed words, we paint bright rainbows,
Tickling our senses like peachy prose.

A banter of biscuits, crumbs scatter around,
In our laughter, the echoes of joy resound,
The world feels lighter, like cake in the air,
As we swap sweet nothings with sprightly affair.

So let's twine our verses, honeyed and bold,
In this syrupy saga, let our tales unfold,
With every soft giggle and word on the breeze,
We create tasty moments that are sure to please.

The Essence of a Stolen Moment

In a hurry, the lips collide,
A sneaky peck we try to hide.
With giggles shared, we start to sway,
While passersby just look our way.

A fruit that's ripe, we swipe and taste,
A zesty bite, oh, what a waste!
Your cheek is sweet, it makes me grin,
As I wipe juice from my chin.

Soft Petals and Chilled Dew

Morning breaks with a cheeky grin,
Dewdrops dance, let the fun begin!
A playfight turns into a tease,
As laughter flows like summer breeze.

Your smile's like nectar, oh so sweet,
Every nibble, a playful treat.
Beneath the sun, we twirl and clash,
With sticky hands, we make a splash.

Juiced Memories of Us

A sweet mishap, a fumble here,
Dripping laughter, what we hold dear.
A pint of joy, we pour like wine,
Each little glance, a secret sign.

Like candy apples shining bright,
You stole my heart, I stole a bite.
With slipping shoes and tangled hair,
We giggle loud without a care.

Colorful Liaisons Under the Sun

Painted cheeks and sticky hands,
In sunny fields where laughter stands.
We run amok, like kids at play,
This fleeting moment, come what may.

Bright blooms scatter on the ground,
Every kiss a joyful sound.
We dance on air, we skip and fly,
With gleeful shouts that touch the sky.

Radiance in a Kiss

When lips collide like fruit in spring,
Sweet juices burst, oh what a fling!
A squishy delight, it's a sticky affair,
With giggles and laughter, we don't have a care.

Candy-coated chaos, oh what a mess,
Syrupy smiles, we smile and confess.
A peck gone wild, we slip and we slide,
A merry dance where our flavors collide.

With each playful nibble, we both start to glow,
Like a summer sunrise, it begins to expand,
Juicy joy bubbles, a radiant show,
In this whimsical moment, we fully understand.

Wipe off the goop, let's laugh out loud,
In sugary bliss, we huddle, we crowd.
The world fades away, just you and I,
With radiant kisses, let's reach for the sky.

Rich Harvest of Emotion

Beneath the moon, berries ripe on the vine,
Our mouths meet in greed, oh isn't it fine?
A crop of delight, we gather up cheer,
With each fruity bite, our laughter's sincere.

Oh, the flavors collide in a tumultuous swirl,
Like a piñata burst, with every twirl.
We munch on the laughter, the sweetness, the zest,
In this harvest of joy, we truly feel blessed.

With a wink and a grin, we share our delight,
A dance of the tongue under soft moonlight.
Enjoying the bounty, we both celebrate,
This rich harvest of emotion, isn't it great?

We'll pickle our moments, this fun will not fade,
Like jellies and jams, forever displayed.
In time's jar we'll treasure, with chuckles and glee,
This harvest of laugh, you and me.

Invitingly Tart

Oh how your lips, so invitingly tart,
Spark joy in my mouth, and dance in my heart.
A squeeze of surprise that tickles my soul,
Like lemons and limes, our mischief's the goal.

With sprightly laughter, we pucker and play,
The zesty concoctions won't fade away.
An explosion of giggles, we sip and we share,
A fizzy sensation hanging in the air.

Let's twist and let's whirl, in this flavor parade,
In this cheeky encounter, our shenanigans invade.
A zest of affection that's wonderfully bright,
With each inviting taste, everything feels right.

So come take a chance, let's savor the spree,
With whispers and chuckles, oh just you and me.
In our frothy concoction of fun and delight,
Together, we sparkle, and everything's bright.

Layers of Desire

Peeling back layers, what's hidden within?
A flavor explosion where giggles begin.
With each tender taste, we dip and we dive,
In a fruity allure, we feel so alive.

Like cake with thick frosting, we layer the fun,
A sprinkle of laughter, when all's said and done.
With whims of desire, we chase and we tease,
In layers of sweetness, we do as we please.

A savory bite, then a splash of surprise,
Turning up the heat, with twinkles in our eyes.
With whispers of mischief, enticing the night,
In layers of desire, everything feels right.

So let's fork into bliss, devour it whole,
In our stack of delight, we flourish and roll.
But don't mind the crumbs that we leave in our wake,
In this merry affair, oh, for fun's sake!

Passion Fruit Reverie

In a garden where flavors play,
Lips smacked like kids with a tray.
Smiles burst like ripe fruits, oh dear!
Sour faces quickly disappear.

Grapes giggle, teasing their friends,
Each bite a burst that never ends.
Laughter dances through the air,
As we savor without a care.

Beneath the sun's warm embrace,
We paint joy on nature's face.
With sticky fingers and bright grins,
The midday feast just begins.

Mangos mock with their cheeky flair,
While pineapples try to out-pair.
Fruit fights leave us all in stitches,
Such fun can cure life's glitches.

A Symphony of Sweetness

Note the rhythm, a fruity beat,
Desires blend, oh what a treat!
Pineapple plucks on a flute so fine,
While berries bounce in a sing-song line.

Lemon zests like a cheeky elf,
Whispering secrets of juicy wealth.
Each hummingbird flutters near,
Dancing to sweetness we hear.

Dates roll in with a strut so bold,
Their funny tales are pure gold.
We giggle at rhythms so wild,
As passions rise, we feel like a child.

In this orchestra, all flavors unite,
Creating a charm that's pure delight.
Each note, a flavor, a joyous flair,
A fruity symphony beyond compare.

Drenched in Delight

Splash of laughter, a juice cascade,
In this chaos, a grand charade.
Watermelon laughs as it spills,
Tickling senses, igniting thrills.

Strawberry giggles with frothy cheer,
Fooling everyone, 'I'm not here!'
Every sip is a teasing jest,
Quenching thirst like a fruity quest.

With citrus rain upon our face,
We dance around like in a race.
Drenched in sweetness, oh what fun,
When we play, we're never done!

Ripe laughter fills the warm air,
Summoning joy without a care.
A picnic where pleasure is rife,
Sipping happiness, that's our life!

Honeyed Hints of Midnight

Under a moon that winks and sighs,
Fruits whisper secrets, truth in disguise.
Peaches flirt in the quiet light,
Their sweetness blooms in the heart of night.

Figs share jokes that are juicy and sly,
While cherries blush with a twinkling eye.
A candlelit feast on this velvet scene,
With whispers of honey, so light and keen.

Giggles float with the sweet perfume,
Flavors rise in a delicate bloom.
A trickling laughter, a playful glide,
On this honeyed journey, let's ride!

With stars joining in, a bright parade,
Every taste becomes a big charade.
In the hush of midnight, we all confess,
Life is simply a fruity mess!

Sips of Desire

In summer's heat, a bold dare,
Strawberry seeds fly through the air.
Lips smacked twice, a giggle burst,
Quenching thirst, oh how it hurts!

With ice in glasses, we toss and twirl,
Fruits collide in a playful swirl.
Each sip a spark, when laughter's around,
A trap set by sweetness, we're all spellbound.

Fingers stained with juice so bright,
Caught in the moment, what a delight!
Echoes of laughter, sticky and bold,
In every swirl, stories unfold.

So raise your cup, let the juices flow,
In this silly dance, we steal the show.
With fruity desires, we twist and we reel,
In this lively game, let's make a meal!

Ripened Hearts

Beneath the tree, secrets are shared,
With ripe banana tricks, oh who dared?
Peeling back layers, blush on our cheeks,
Flavorful giggles, oh how it peaks!

Mango mischief, a slippery bite,
Fumbling fingers, oh what a sight!
Juicy explosions, sweet on the tongue,
In this wild feast, we laugh and we run.

Cantaloupe kisses, a taste divine,
Fruit by fruit, our hearts intertwine.
Cherries collide, a comic embrace,
In juicy antics, we find our place.

Sharing delights, a fruit basket charm,
Wrapped in laughter, all safe from harm.
In ripened hearts, we're bound to soar,
With every bite, who could want more?

Flavors of Longing

Pineapple dreams cut into stars,
Sweetness lingers like melody bars.
Tickling tongues with a burst of zest,
In flavors of longing, we find our rest.

Dancing grapes tumble from our hands,
Spilling wishes like grains of sands.
Sipping nectar, we giggle and sway,
In this fruity dance, we're led astray.

Raspberry ripples spark playful delight,
As we toast to the sounds of the night.
Fruity whispers, a tasty tease,
In sweet little moments, we aim to please.

Give me a splash, a dash of charm,
With every flavor, we mean no harm.
In this garden of taste, we're captivated,
With juice on our lips, we feel elated!

Cravings Unleashed

Tangerine giggles spill on the ground,
In a wet and wild fruit playground.
With fingers sticky, we summon the sun,
Each zesty bite, oh what a fun!

Avocado antics mix with delight,
Creamy chaos, oh what a sight!
Like dashing raindrops that dance in the cake,
In cravings unleashed, we happily shake.

Chasing fruits 'round, with glee in our eyes,
Sipping delights, beneath cotton skies.
What a concoction, a silly parade,
In joyful laughter, our worries will fade.

Ripe inspirations pile up on plates,
Mischief with fruit, oh love, it creates!
So gather your friends, let the feast begin,
In this juicy madness, we all dive in!

Ripe Moments of Heartfelt Joy

In a garden of laughter, we beam,
Chasing shadows, a whimsical dream.
Our smiles burst like bubbles in air,
Sweet memories linger, we dance without care.

With each giggle, the world feels bright,
Banana peels fly, a comical sight.
A splash of jelly on buttered bread,
We feast on joy, and giggles we spread.

Laughter ripples like a flowing stream,
Moments like these feel far from a scheme.
Wobbly walks on a playground swing,
In the folly of fun, our hearts take wing.

When tickled by sunshine, we play our part,
Jumping in puddles, we'll never depart.
Together we savor these bright little joys,
In this merry universe, we are the toys.

Flavors of Forever Entwined

A sunshine splash with a twist of lime,
Life's a buffet, let's sip on sweet thyme.
Sharing tastes of laughter, we twirl and spin,
With each goofy grin, we dare to begin.

Chocolate fountains pour from the skies,
Sundae dreams with cherry surprise.
With sprinkles of joy, we paint the day,
Each flavor entangled in a delightful play.

Soda pop fizz, it tickles the tongue,
In the chorus of fun, we happily sung.
Epic taste battles, we challenge with glee,
The winner is laughter, so wild and free.

Our fingers sticky from candies and sweets,
Creating a mess, it's a joyous feat.
Life's flavors blend in a whimsical swirl,
Hand in hand, let's give the world a twirl.

Lips Like Ripe Berries

Berry bright kisses that shimmer and gleam,
Laughter on lips, a whimsical dream.
Red as a rose, they twinkle and tease,
Cheeky moments that tickle with ease.

Juicy delights that burst in the night,
In the game of giggles, we both take flight.
Lapping up joy like sweet summer rain,
No sweeter concoction, it eases the pain.

With each tiny peck, we stir up the fun,
Strolling through parks, two hearts have begun.
Unruly adventures, on stilts we shall prance,
In berry-bright chaos, we twirl and we dance.

Oh, the tastes that make clowns of us all,
With every sweet snack, we rise and we fall.
Lips like ripe berries, they frolic and play,
In the garden of laughter, we brighten the day.

Savoring Sweet Silences

In quiet stillness, we share our treat,
A slice of pie, oh, the joy we meet.
Moments of silence are rarely bland,
With a sprinkle of laughter, together we stand.

The crunch of sugar and playful sighs,
We savor the silence, our spirits rise.
A wink across the table, giggles ignite,
In this blissful hush, everything feels right.

A luscious cake with frosting so bright,
We savor each moment, a pure delight.
With eyes that twinkle, we playfully beam,
In the language of silence, we share our dream.

As napkins crinkle and voices stay low,
Flavors of friendship are bound to grow.
In this sweet silence, we find the fun,
An echo of laughter from two become one.

Forbidden Flavors Collide

In the market, fruits collide,
A citrus laugh, and passion's ride.
One bite leads to sweet confusion,
Taste buds dance in wild conclusion.

Raspberry winks at lime's bold shout,
Peach blushes while grape spins about.
Together they spark a playful fight,
Creating chaos, oh what a sight!

Mango teases, 'Why not taste?'
Kissing flavors, no time to waste.
Cherries giggle, 'What would they think?'
Syrup spills, they start to clink!

In this fruity, charming mess,
Laughter reigns, oh what a stress.
Let's savor these bites of pure delight,
In forbidden flavors, we'll take flight!

Berry-Stained Promises

Under moonlight, berries gleam,
Whispers sweet, living the dream.
Juicy secrets hide in leaves,
Making promises, oh how they tease!

Strawberries share a naughty grin,
Wishing that the thrill would begin.
Blueberries giggle, their cheeks so round,
In this berry bush, joy is found.

Tangled up on a picnic rug,
Hands get sticky, feeling the tug.
Laughter spills from every bite,
Berry-stained lips, pure delight.

Under stars, we share our tales,
A raucous charm that never fails.
With every tangy, sweet embrace,
Berry promises—what a taste!

Velvet Touch of Desire

Velvet petals in twilight's grasp,
A touch so soft, we start to gasp.
In the garden, whispers bloom,
Sweetened nectar fills the room.

Honey drips in playful streams,
As flavors burst from vivid dreams.
Lemon zest and chocolate swirls,
Dancing close, a taste of pearls.

In this moment, time stands still,
A frolic of flavors, such a thrill.
Laughter echoes, a gentle tease,
In this sweet embrace, hearts freeze.

With every bite, desire sings,
In the air, a spark that clings.
Velvet kisses, oh how they shine,
A whimsical dance, your hand in mine!

Exquisite Flavor of Longing

With each longing glance, we play,
Flavorful dreams in light of day.
Grapefruit wishes, tart and bright,
A taste of passion, pure delight.

Peachy nibbles lead to sighs,
Underneath a canvas of skies.
Whipped cream clouds float overhead,
As sweet nothings are gently said.

Cherries pop with a teasing pout,
Gathering laughter as we shout.
Each flavor pulls, a gleeful tug,
Tasting moments, oh how they hug!

Through every kiss, the flavors blend,
An exquisite longing that won't end.
In this banquet of hearts, we cheer,
Every sip shared, oh so dear!

Drenched in Ecstasy

The fruit fell just right, oh what a sight,
With juice on my chin, it sparked sheer delight.
In a clumsy embrace, we both made a mess,
Sticky fingers and laughter, here's to the jest!

A mischievous grin, as pulp flies about,
We giggle and wiggle, with nothing to pout.
Sweet dribbles of fun, oh what a delight,
In this wild summer day, we took our first bite.

Wearing fruit salad, we dance in the sun,
With juice-splattered clothes, this day's just begun.
Mix flavors of joy, let's play on repeat,
With every fresh nibble, life's oh so sweet!

So raise up your hands, embrace fruity charms,
In this zany love feast, we'll share our warm arms.
No need for romance, just laughter and zest,
Together we savor, we sure are the best!

Fluttering Flavors

A touch of citrus brings forth a grin,
With every juicy pop, we both dive in.
Lemonade laughter and fruity high fives,
Together we shimmer and come so alive.

Berry kisses, oh what a taste,
With each playful bite, we'll never go to waste.
A carnival swirl, oh how we can prance,
Every nibble feels like a silly romance.

Tropical giggles, pineapple bliss,
A good-natured squabble, here's a sweet kiss.
Oh, don't mind the chaos, the juice will run free,
In this joyful buffet, just you and me.

So toss out the napkins, let's savor the fun,
With flavor explosions, we'll never outrun.
In this feast of delight, let the flavors collide,
With laughter and sweetness, let's dance side by side!

Supple Connections

Strawberry flirtations, so ripe and so bold,
With succulent bites, our stories unfold.
Mango mischief, oh how it drips,
We savor sweet moments that dance on our lips.

Each nibble brings laughter, a funny refrain,
Juicy confessions, like sunshine after rain.
In our slippery game, let's take one more bite,
With giggles and grins, everything feels right.

Fruit-filled adventures, oh how they delight,
With sticky connections, we'll hold on tight.
No ordinary snack, this playful pursuit,
In this blend of flavors, our friendship takes root.

So toss down those worries, let's dip and let dive,
In this fruity assembly, our spirits will thrive.
With playful connections, we burst into song,
In this festival of flavor, we truly belong!

Fruit of Enchantment

Sliced up imagination, ripe on our plate,
We nibble in laughter, oh, isn't it great?
Each taste an adventure, a giggly mistake,
Barefoot on grass, let's dance for the sake.

Cherry chuckles and kiwi delight,
A tangle of sweetness in soft morning light.
With each juicy bite, we're a messy delight,
Our laughter erupts as we take a big bite.

Peachy sensations, they light up the air,
With giggles and juice dribbling everywhere.
Let's blend up the fun, take a fruity chance,
With playful enchantments, we spin and we dance.

So gather your friends, let's share in this feast,
In this whimsical world, let's party at least.
With flavor explosions and happy bliss,
This fruity adventure, we'll surely not miss!

Flavors that Linger

Lemon drops and bubble gum,
Sour faces, but here's some fun.
Cherry lips with raspberry swirl,
A taste explosion makes us twirl.

Minty fresh with a dash of glee,
Giggles mixed with syrupy spree.
Fruit punch dreams and cotton candy,
A playful mix that feels quite dandy.

Whipped cream kisses on a summer's day,
Sticky fingers lead us astray.
Chocolate smirks and confetti sprinkles,
Every peck a sweet little twinkle.

Lasting flavors, a cheeky tease,
We savor this—just like we'd please.
In the land of taste, we can't resist,
Each kiss a flavor, oh such bliss!

Celestial Cravings

Stars align with chocolate moons,
Crispy comets and candy tunes.
Cosmic flavors dance in the air,
Every kiss a proof of care.

Banana boats on a milky way,
Giggles orbiting, brightening the day.
Sugar crystals on starry nights,
Kisses sweet like sparkling lights.

Peanut butter planets, oh what fun,
In our universe, we are one.
Galactic whimsies, sugar rush,
Silly faces, we're in a hush.

In this space where laughter glows,
Every kiss a universe that flows.
Dreamy flavors in cosmic array,
Keep us floating, come what may!

Aroma of Affection

Basil breath and garlic tease,
Chasing love with fragrant ease.
Honey drips and citrus smiles,
Our hearts are flowing through the miles.

Scented candles and spicy chats,
Whiffs of laughter, silly spats.
Savory whispers, oh so sweet,
Every kiss a special treat.

Rosemary skies and thyme-y breezes,
Tickling noses, love that pleases.
Tasty hugs in a cozy mix,
Jumbles of joy in funny tricks.

A splash of zest, a pinch of cheer,
Every moment, my dear, so clear.
With every embrace that fills the air,
We find our scent, a perfect pair!

Sun-Kissed Passion

Sunshine beams and warming rays,
Tickled toes on lazy days.
Lemonade cups and playful splashes,
Every kiss is just like candy crashes.

With surfboards and bright beach balls,
Sandy toes and laughter calls.
Jellyfish dance, whimsically float,
Every peck is like a happy note.

Breezy waves and sunshine's glow,
Tropical tunes in the ebb and flow.
Fruitful kisses with berry fun,
We're surfing joy, just having fun.

Under the sun where giggles blend,
Every oh-so-naughty trend.
Passionate warmth wrapped in zest,
In this bloom, we feel the best!

Cherry Blossom Embrace

In springtime's wake, a gentle breeze,
Petals swirl down like a sneeze.
Two lovers giggle in the park,
Chasing blossoms until it's dark.

Abe's so clumsy, he trips on grass,
Luna laughs, "You're such a champ!
Your face is red, you look a sight!"
Their jokes bloom like flowers in light.

A bouquet of giggles fills the air,
His attempts at charm, a crazy dare.
With every mishap, their hearts unfold,
A love story painted in pink and gold.

As cherries hang ripe in the sun,
They share a laugh, two hearts as one.
Together they dance, no hint of shame,
In their cherry blossom love game.

Pomegranate Dreams Exploded

At the party, things got wild,
With pomegranate juice, they both smiled.
A splash here, a squirt there,
On everything, chaos everywhere.

Tom tried to flirt, a juice-filled grin,
But ended up with stains on his chin.
"Hey, nice shot!" Sally couldn't help but say,
As red juice decorated his buffet.

With laughter echoing through the space,
The pomegranate stains became their grace.
"What a night!" they both proclaimed,
In sticky sweetness, love was named.

As juicy memories filled the room,
They waved goodbye to any gloom.
Their hearts, like seeds, in a fruity jest,
Came together in a colorful quest.

Molten Sugar on a Summer Night

Beneath the stars, they took a seat,
With sticky hands, their love's so sweet.
Ice cream melting, laughter rings,
Cinnamon swirls and sugar flings.

Mike took a bite, but oh, what a scene,
Splat! Ice cream lands on Brenda's jeans.
"Now we match!" she laughs with glee,
Two messy souls, as happy as can be.

In the glow of summer's warm embrace,
They share a sundae, a sugary race.
With cherries on top, their hearts align,
Using straws to sip from the same divine.

As midnight strikes, they can't resist,
A sugar high, they can't dismiss.
In melted joy, they leave their plight,
With hearts so full, it feels just right.

Citrus Caress Under Moonlight

On a summer night, lemons float,
A zestful dance in a tiny boat.
With grabs of oranges, a fruit-filled spree,
Squeezing laughter from every tree.

Jake, the joker, slipped on a rind,
"Look at me!" he laughed, quite unrefined.
Lime wedges bounced in a fruity fright,
As they rolled under the soft moonlight.

Zesty tricks in the cool night air,
Maddie spun round, calling "Come over, dear!"
With citrus kisses, they twirl with glee,
In a citrus-infused reverie.

Lemonade dreams fill their hearts with cheer,
As they giggle about their playful sphere.
Underneath the moon's loving embrace,
They find a spark in this citrus chase.

Blissful Bursts

In the kitchen, charm takes flight,
With flavors bold, oh what a sight!
A laugh erupts with every taste,
A silly dance, no time to waste.

Lemon twirls with cheeky glee,
Orange giggles, wild and free.
Sweet surprises, oh what fun,
A fruity mishap, everyone run!

Cherry chuckles, it won't stop,
Splashing juice like a soda pop.
They hold a party in my mouth,
Turning laughter north and south.

The blender's whir, a merry tune,
Fruit frolics beneath the moon.
A slip, a spill, a cheeky grin,
In this zesty, fruity din!

Lush Caresses

Grapes are squished, oh, what delight,
Juicy dribbles in the night.
A friendly duel with peppy zest,
Who can take the silliest guess?

Plum and peach, they frolic near,
Whispering tales we all can hear.
A slippery dance on floors so slick,
Watch your step, it's all a trick!

Mango giggles, what a tease,
Sticky fingers made with ease.
This fruity game, we'll laugh and play,
Until the sun takes us away.

Kiwi winks, a secret shared,
Split us open, none are spared.
A burst of joy, a riotous cheer,
In this luscious mess, we've nothing to fear!

Strawberry Stolen

A basket placed, what's that I see?
Berries winking right at me!
One quick taste, a sneaky bite,
Giggles echo into the night.

Naughty red with spotted flair,
Who knew trouble lurked right there?
Tickled taste buds, oh what bliss,
Each berry bears a juicy kiss.

Chubby cheeks and sticky hands,
Exploring flavor's merry lands.
A daring chase, we dash and dart,
Stolen sweets, a cheeky art.

The fruit parade rolls down the lane,
A splatter splash, a sugar rain.
We burst with laughter, oh so bold,
In every bite, a tale retold!

Honey Dripped Wishes

With honey drips and sticky fate,
I take a scoop, can hardly wait.
A spoonful slips, it's quite a scene,
Sweetness laughing like a queen.

Wishing wells with nectar's charms,
Caught in flavors, oh, such alarms.
A drizzle here, a puddle there,
Sticky fingers everywhere!

Cinnamon twirls with a cheeky kiss,
Swirls of sweetness, purest bliss.
Imagine dreams on toast so light,
In sticky giggles, hearts take flight.

Laughter pours like syrup slow,
How many spoons can one bestow?
Under blooms of honey sighs,
Each taste a burst, a grand surprise!

www.ingramcontent.com/pod-product-compliance
Lightning Source LLC
Chambersburg PA
CBHW060115230426
43661CB00003B/192